C000143692

Hugh Dodd
Dick Hamilton

A GOOD
WIGGING

Dedicated to Sara Lise Dodd

Hugh Dodd
Dick Hamilton

A GOOD WIGGING

Butterworths

United Kingdom	Butterworth & Co (Publishers) Ltd, 88 Kingsway, LONDON WC2B 6AB and 61A North Castle Street, EDINBURGH EH2 3LJ
Australia	Butterworths Pty Ltd, SYDNEY, MELBOURNE, BRISBANE, ADELAIDE, PERTH, CANBERRA and HOBART
Canada	Butterworths Canada Ltd, TORONTO and VANCOUVER
Ireland	Butterworth (Ireland) Ltd, DUBLIN
Malaysia	Malayan Law Journal Sdn Bhd, KUALA LUMPUR
New Zealand	Butterworths of New Zealand Ltd, WELLINGTON and AUCKLAND
Singapore	Butterworth & Co (Asia) Pte Ltd, SINGAPORE
USA	Butterworths Legal Publishers, ST PAUL, Minnesota, SEATTLE, Washington, BOSTON, Massachusetts, AUSTIN, Texas and D & S Publishers CLEARWATER, Florida

All rights reserved. No part of this publication may be reproduced or transmitted in any form or by any means (including photocopying and recording) without the written permission of the copyright holder except in accordance with the provisions of the Copyright Act 1956 (as amended) or under the terms of a licence issued by the Copyright Licensing Agency, 7 Ridgemount Street, London, England WC1E 7AE. The written permission of the copyright holder must also be obtained before any part of this publication is stored in a retrieval system of any nature. Applications for the copyright holder's written permission to reproduce, transmit or store in a retrieval system any part of this publication should be addressed to the publisher.

Warning: The doing of an unauthorised act in relation to a copyright work may result in both a civil claim for damages and criminal prosecution.

© Butterworth & Co (Publishers) Ltd 1988

© Hugh Dodd 1988

A CIP Catalogue record for this book is available from the British Library

ISBN 0 406 50990 5

Printed by Lawrence-Allen Limited, Weston-super-Mare

Foreword

Having spent my life in the practice of the law I find it most refreshing that an observant eye should be cast over us and that the resulting impressions should be drawn by the hand of a skilful artist. This may give us some insight into the way that 'others see us' but perhaps even more important it enables us to discern things about ourselves and the way we conduct our business which, but for the artist's intervention, we might not have noticed.

I am sure that the 16 upright images drawn by Hugh Dodd will give all who have practised the law, according to the British tradition, a great deal of amusement as well as enabling them to notice things about what they do and the people with whom they deal, that they have not previously noticed.

When these pictures are accompanied by such appropriate text, prepared by a lawyer having the experience of His Honour Judge Richard Hamilton, whose talents lie not only in the law but in writing and broadcasting, the publishers are to be congratulated on an arrangement amounting to a really good wigging for the law. The presentation and format is equal to the artistic skill displayed in the contents and the book will, I am sure, give pleasure to many interested in the law whether they have practised it themselves or not.

Mackay of Clashfern

Point of Departure

Five centuries ago, Leonardo da Vinci made some observations upon the human countenance.

'If you want to acquire facility for bearing in mind the expression of a face', he wrote, 'first make yourself familiar with a variety of forms of several heads, eyes, noses, mouths, chins and cheeks and necks and shoulders. And to put a case: noses are of 10 types; straight, bulbous, hollow, prominent above or below the middle, aquiline, regular, flat, rounded or pointed...'

Many famous artists have been fascinated by the human condition, whether drawing in sympathy or caricature. They include Thomas Rowlandson, William Hogarth, Henri Daumier, and George Cruickshank, the beloved 'Phiz' of Charles Dickens' works.

Now Hugh Dodd has turned his attention to the legal profession, and what better? When Dickens described Samuel Pickwick's trial at the Guildhall for breach of promise of marriage, there were:

'A numerous muster of gentlemen in wigs, in the barristers' seats: who represented, as a body, all that pleasing and extensive variety of nose and whisker for which the Bar of England is so justly celebrated.'

Some people might think it unseemly to caricature the legal profession. However, the Lord Chancellor, Lord Mackay of Clashfern, had this to say in a recent case:

'But law is a practical affair and has to approach its problems in a mundane commonsense way. We cannot expect always to have a tidy and interrelated picture; in real life a surrealistic element is apt to creep in, and the picture, though untidy and unharmonious, is a picture all the same.'

If the following pictures have their occasional surrealistic moments, they also have their moments of truth.

I

The Mighty Judge

At home he is an absolute darling. He sits his granddaughter on his knee, and reads her *Winnie-the-Pooh*; he cultivates superb roses. But in court he is a different man, with his hard-boiled eyes, and crusty voice ripened with port like a Stilton cheese.

Dostoevsky, who in *The House of the Dead* described several years as a political prisoner in a Siberian prison camp, wrote:

> 'I know strange examples of honourable men, kindly and esteemed by all their friends, who yet saw fit to have a culprit whipped until he begged for mercy; it seemed quite natural to them, a measure to be recognised as indispensable.'

A more alarming view of a criminal judge was voiced by one of the characters in Agatha Christie's *Ten Little Niggers*:

> 'To begin with, he's an old man and he's been presiding over courts of law for years. That is to say, he's played God Almighty for a good many months every year. That must go to a man's head eventually...
> — and it's possible that his brain might snap...'

But judges' brains are seldom as fragile as that. If the judge is formidable, it is because his task is formidable; he tackles formidable problems, argued by formidable advocates. In the criminal court, he deals with some of the ugliest forms of evil that can be imagined, facing details of which most citizens remain happily ignorant.

The wisest view of his duties was perhaps expressed by Goethe in *Faust*:

> 'The Judge who cannot punish crime
> joins with the culprit in the court.'

The Mighty Judge

Femme Fatale

'What a formidable influence women have on the history of nations!' wrote the great Spanish writer Galdos, charting the progress of his nation. 'Men, by thought, lay down theories and systems, and form parties; women, by love or hate, determine the action. If one considers history as a drama, man is the actor, and woman the author. There has never been a great historical event which has not gone down into history urged on by feminine hands, and the ship of state so often mentioned in political articles would most often never have set sail without being towed by the swift doves of Venus.'

This is not an universal rule, but it certainly applies to the woman in the witness box. She may once have been a fresh-cheeked maiden, but success and money and ambition have whetted her character till it has a fine cutting edge. Lady Sackville once got the better even of the great F E Smith, at the height of his career.

'Her methods as a witness', wrote her daughter, Vita Sackville-West, 'I need hardly say were completely irregular. The ingenuity she displayed in evading any question she didn't want to answer was a triumph of femininity at its best and worst. She was disconcerting, maddening, witty. At moments she had the whole court in roars of laughter, when even the judge permitted himself a smile. For one thing she insisted on treating FE as a person she knew socially, as indeed she did. Sometimes she appealed direct to the judge.

"My Lord, may I ask you something? My Lord, you may remember, and the gentlemen of the jury —"

FE (wearily): "I will sit down." '

So the woman in the witness box lords it over counsel, and the judge, and anyone else who stands in her way. Such women have existed since the dawn of time. As a proverb put it from Ancient Babylon, 'For his pleasure — married. On thinking it over — divorced.'

Femme Fatale

Life's Theatre

In the artificial drama of the law, it is a mysterious but rigid rule of etiquette that barristers *do not shake hands*. So it has to be something pretty important to make barristers overlook that tradition. Perhaps they have got an adjournment. To quote an old ballad,

'Methought I saw two lawyers base
    One to another say
We have had in hand this poore man's case
    a twelve month and a day:
And yet we'll not contented be
    to let the matter fall
Bear thou with me, & I'll beare with thee
    While poore men pay for all'.

Delay is now classified as one of the abuses of the court which can give rise to judicial review, as was considered when an important bypass was held up for several years.

'Two and a half years had elapsed', said Lord Justice Woolf. 'The delay was caused by these proceedings. It was to be deplored especially because the proceedings were manifestly without merit...But it should be added that despite the strong criticism of the way that the applications were made, neither counsel nor solicitors for the applicants had intended to abuse the process of the court.'

Are lawyers the worst offenders in matters of delay? Probably not. Karen Blixen, in her famous book *Out of Africa*, said of a particular tribe many years ago, 'One can always impress a Native by wasting more time over a matter than he does himself, only it is a very difficult thing to accomplish.'

Still, to err is human, to adjourn divine. As has been wisely observed, 'The best labour-saving device of today is still tomorrow.'

VI

Life's Theatre

Time is Money

The storm in a teacup has reached gale force.

'And everyone *knows* that Mrs McGrowther always stops her car so that the exhaust fumes ruin my petunias', says Miss Twistle anxiously, reaching for a tiny handkerchief. 'These are *facts*.'

'Quite so', says learned counsel; but time is money. He secretly presses the button which sounds a buzzer in the clerks' room. In a minute or two he will be told that the Government wishes to consult with him on a matter of national security. He brings the consultation to an end most reluctantly, it being obvious that the problems of her herbaceous border weigh heavily upon his mind.

So she goes away happily. He could have told her not to waste his time, but she needs kindness even more than her tranquillisers. Perhaps some means can be found of guiding her gently in a different direction before she spends too much money on the case. Everything depends on his smooth, light touch; hypocrisy is too harsh a word.

It is a delicate balance. He can maintain the illusion so long as it is based on his superior skill and knowledge. But clients are not supposed to be a match for their counsel. They might not defer to him, and he would certainly not take kindly to it. Two of Charles Dickens' characters realised this:

'"They're always a-bringing up some new law or other."

"And according to what I was reading you in the paper the other day, father, what the Judge said, you know, we poor people are supposed to know them all. Ha, ha! What a mistake! My goodness, how clever they'd think us!"

"Yes, my dear", said Trotty, "and they'd be very fond of anyone of us that *did* know 'em all!"'

Time is Money

Prosecuting Counsel

Junior counsel for the Crown has an admiration bordering on worship of his eminent leader; this makes them a well-matched pair, since his leader shares that view of his talents. Yet when he rises to conduct a devastating cross-examination, who is at risk?

'A reputation for specialising in prosecuting puts a man in a precarious situation, and has an adverse effect on his good name', wrote Cicero. 'There is no need, on the other hand, to have any scruples about occasionally defending a person who is guilty — provided that he is not really a depraved or wicked character. For popular sentiment requires this; it is sanctioned by custom, and conforms with human decency.'

It is surprising he should think so, since his triumphant prosecution of Verres, a corrupt Roman governor, was the start of his brilliant career. Popular opinion expects a prosecutor to be lethally effective. In Anthony Trollope's novels, however, it was usually the defence counsel who played the more dominant role:

'He would ask a few civil little questions, in his softest voice, glaring out of his wicked old eye as he did so at those around him, and then, when he had his mouse well in hand, out would come his envenomed claw, and the wretched animal would feel the fatal wound in his tenderest part...

He bullies when it is quite unnecessary that he should bully; it is a labour of love; and though he is now old, and stiff in his joints, though ease would be dear to him, though like a gladiator satiated with blood, he would as regards himself be so pleased to sheathe his sword, yet he never spares himself. He never spares himself, and he never spares his victim.'

At the Old Bailey, R D Muir never spared himself or his victim; he prosecuted Crippen and many other famous murderers. His painstaking work never missed a single detail, and his presentation of cases was always firm and fair. A sensational style would have horrified him.

Such are the highest traditions of the Bar.

Prosecuting Counsel

Enter the Clerk

On your right, the Duchess of Barset; she has just won her claim for half a million pounds. On your left, the eminent counsel who has steered her case to success. She invites him and his wife to stay the weekend at her stately home, and with an excellent show of diffidence, he accepts. So far, so good; but an important stage direction appears in this scene: Enter the Clerk.

'Excuse me, sir', says Sid with all the deference of Jeeves holding sway over Bertie Wooster, 'but Mr Mumbles needs an urgent conference in the Mexican Weevil case. Saturday afternoon, sir. — No, sir, you haven't seen the papers, sir. That's why he needs the conference, sir. — Sorry to upset your arrangements, sir, but Mr Mumbles is a new client. — Could be important, sir. Case might go to the House of Lords.'

Is it seriously to be supposed that Sid, a mere clerk, can dominate one of the most eminent men at the Bar? Certainly, for both of them are programmed to this way of life. When the great man was a raw novice at the Bar, Sid passed his first briefs into his trembling hands, and nursed his career against early frosts.

Henry Hawkins, one of the greatest advocates of Victorian times, knew from the start where his interests lay.

'Hundreds of times', he recalled, 'had I listened with vain expectations to the footsteps on the stairs below — footsteps of attorneys and clerks, messengers and office-boys. Down below at the bottom flight they tramped, and there they mostly stopped.' (He was on the fifth floor.)

'The ground floor was evidently the best for business; but some came higher, to the first floor. That was a good position, there were plenty of footsteps, and I could tell they were the footsteps of clients...

Now someone had come up to the third floor; he stopped! Alas!'

To him, a clerk with a brief would have been like an angel from heaven. His whole future depended on that simple phrase: Enter the Clerk.

Enter the Clerk

The Young Demosthenes

Young Mr Hopeful, in his brand-new wig, robes and suit, stands in front of the mirror, reflecting on the 'glittering prizes of the Bar', as F E Smith called them, which he knows must immediately come his way.

'Say I could succeed at the Bar', said the young hero of Thackeray's *Pendennis*, 'and achieve a fortune by bullying witnesses and twisting evidence; is that a fame which would satisfy my longings, or a calling in which my life would be well spent?'

Those are not Mr Hopeful's doubts. He will never bully witnesses; he is sure of that. A few masterly questions to them will demolish their cases like a pack of cards. What, though, of pernickety arguments? Seneca, the great Roman philosopher, and a lawyer, despised them.

'Is this the way to our supreme ideal?' he wrote. 'Do we get there by means of all that "if X, Y, or if not Y, Z" one finds in philosophy? And by means of quibbles that would be shameful and discreditable even among persons occupying themselves with law reports?'

Mr Hopeful will maintain a soul entirely above such things, until a string of twopenny-halfpenny cases, of no seeming merit, forces him to take piffling points, for want of anything better on his client's behalf.

Gradually he will come to see that there is more to be said for his plodding colleagues than he was prepared to admit. Meanwhile, his blissful inexperience is as untouched as the bloom on a freshly picked bunch of grapes. The crustiest old judges observe him as he embarks upon a career of adventure, and remember their own successes and disasters. If he knew how much they both envy him and wish him well, he would be agreeably surprised.

The Young Demosthenes

The Conference

Mrs Mayson-Fortinham was born with a silver spoon in her mouth; when she first saw the light, it was a chandelier. Since then the world has owed her a lavish living, and a better husband than the present, and fourth, holder of that title.

Mr Catchpole, her divorce barrister, inquires what went wrong in the marriage.

'What can I say about Reggie?' she murmurs. 'He was just — impossible.'

'But in what way? Was it drink?' She tosses her head. 'Violence?' Another toss. 'Sex?' A shudder of distaste.

'All I can say is, he was just impossible', she repeats. How she managed to have three children without spoiling her coiffure, is difficult to conceive.

'For a lawyer to fall in love with a pretty client on a single consultation', wrote Sir Walter Scott, 'would be as wise as if he became enamoured of a particularly bright sunbeam which chanced for a moment to gild his Bar wig.'

This is not Mr Catchpole's temptation. He would like to get home to his wife in Surbiton, with Lancashire hot-pot for supper. He is wondering whether a barrister has ever murdered a client, and proved justifiable homicide.

James Boswell, whose intimate knowledge of women went beyond his long-suffering wife, reckoned that marriages would in general be as happy, and even more so, if they were all made by the Lord Chancellor. There is certainly a case for legal control; Mrs Mayson-Fortinham should be disqualified from holding a marriage licence for the period of five years.

But men find her irresistible, and another poor devil will soon fall into her clutches. As a Japanese proverb puts it, 'Every worm to his taste; some prefer nettles.'

The Conference

Plea in Mitigation

Standing, so to speak, behind his client, counsel launches into an impassioned plea on his behalf, and leaves no cliché unturned. His client's life was tragically deprived, he says; he could not even afford a television or microwave oven. (That is why he borrows other people's, at dead of night.)

If only his Lordship will grant his client 'one final chance', his client knows that it will be the 'very last'. His girl-friend is about to give birth to their seventh child, and he would dearly treasure the chance to be present at that touching event. (On previous occasions he was drunk in the pub by way of anaesthetic, but counsel does not mention this.)

Whilst his character is being whitewashed, as it were, in glowing colours, the defendant turns upon the court a smile of practised charm that any second-hand car salesman would envy. Once the court has taken 36 other offences of burglary into consideration, he is prepared to 'turn over a new leaf' and re-enter society with hardly a 'stain on his character'.

His client, says counsel, is deeply ashamed of the position in which he finds himself. (Which is true; no self-respecting burglar should have left his fingerprints on the window-pane.) Now his client 'stands at the crossroads of his career'; but the judge's face suggests that all roads lead to gaol.

Finally, counsel invites the judge to give his client a sentence which can be 'measured in months' rather than 'years'.

The Judge, always willing to oblige, sends the defendant down for 60 months.

Plea in Mitigation

Presenting a Bold Front

George Orwell's literary tastes were wide and varied. He rejoiced in the naughty seaside postcards of Donald McGill, not least the one of a scene in court:

> '*Judge*: You are prevaricating, sir. Did you or did you not sleep with this woman?
>
> *Co-Respondent*: Not a wink, my Lord!'

When the jollier forms of immorality collide with the law, it is not always easy to keep a straight face. There was a time when women were only allowed to appear naked on stage provided they stood stock still; when burly police constables raided night-clubs, and gave shocked evidence of how the girls took their clothes off. If there is ever a swing of the moral pendulum, these long-forgotten scenes could be with us once again.

But love laughs at locksmiths, and lust at legislators. Unhappy is the lot of those who try to define immorality, however worthy the intentions or pressing the need. Breast springs eternal in the human hope, and most forms of censorship are in the end self-defeating. Baroness Wootton of Abinger gave a striking example from her own experience.

> 'I remember sitting as a magistrate at Bow Street to hear a charge of selling obscene postcards, and the learned clerk looked up a reference and advised the court that when such articles were confiscated they must be sold and the proceeds go to defray the costs of the proceedings.'

But should naughty films have to be considered in detail, the key textbook on the work of magistrates' courts, *Stone's Justices' Manual*, lays down the procedure:

> 'Where it is necessary to show indecent films, the public can be excluded from any showing, but not the Press.'

It is reassuring to know that reporters, as well as magistrates, are immune to what might be bad for most of us.

Presenting a Bold Front

The Fox

He walks away from the court having won yet another seemingly hopeless case, and looks mightily pleased with himself; he will sleep well tonight.

'I think that conscience in businessmen is a bit like virginity in whores', said someone in a Spanish novel; '— they sell it when they haven't got it any more. Hardly anybody in business has a conscience, because they've heard it's likely to get in your way. So they leave it behind with their umbilical cords when they're born.'

Is he, then, to stand beside the shyster lawyer in the American film of whom it was said 'he could even find a loophole in the Ten Commandments'? Yes and no. He stoops to no fraud, and conceals no material facts. But if there is a loophole in the Ten Commandments, he finds it for his client, and his ingenuity is at the service of great causes as well as bad ones. Hence his success, which is by no means to be despised.

'I hasten to say', ruled Lord Justice Croom-Johnson in a case where a determined barrister clashed with a coroner at a controversial inquest, 'that there is no suggestion that he behaved improperly in any way. Not all his points were good, particularly in relation to the production and use of documents, and he was persistent. But counsel are there to be persistent, always provided that they realise when to stop.'

'The most useful lawyers, as a rule', wrote Anthony Trollope in his autobiography, 'have been those who have made the greatest incomes — and it is the same with doctors.' So our hero pursues his highly remunerative career. If he has one fault, he shares the same lack of lofty ideals as a character in Gogol's *The Nose*:

'There's nothing finer than bank-notes', he used to say, 'they don't need feeding, take up very little room and slip nicely into the pocket. And they don't break if you drop them.'

The Fox

A Good Result

Every picture tells a story. The weeping woman, if you like, leaves the court a tragic victim of the legal system.

'Lawyers seldom part with so good a cause', wrote J Arbuthnot in 1712, 'till they have got the oyster, and their clients the shell.'

Meanwhile, the barristers look on impassively. 'A lawyer's anxiety about the fate of the most interesting case', observed Sir Walter Scott, 'has seldom spoiled either his sleep or his digestion.'

But the picture may not be all that it appears. Some old ladies persist in ruinously expensive litigation despite the most heroic efforts on the part of their legal advisers to stop them. Sir Walter Scott noted in his *Journal*,

> 'There is something sickening in seeing poor devils drawn into great expense about trifles by interested attorneys. But too cheap access to litigation has its evils on the other side, for the proneness of the lower class to gratify spite and revenge in this way would be a dreadful evil were they able to endure the expense.'

Today the legal aid system goes a great way to help the poor, so that they can fight cases of merit. But there will always be tragic cases of those who could have accepted a reasonable settlement, but went on greedily for more, and lost everything. There will also be those whose obstinate insistence on 'their rights' becomes an obsession. They haunt the courts with sheaves of tattered papers in their hands.

No legal system in the world is free from fault. But, as Lord Simon of Glaisdale observed in a famous case, 'The rule of law is not to be equated with the reign of litigiousness.'

A Good Result

Procrastination

'If only you knew how much I have to do! ...apart from all my other work, — people fall, as if they were drunk, off scaffolds and into machines, all the planks tip up, there are landslides everywhere, all the ladders slip, everything one puts up falls down, and what one puts down one falls over oneself. All these young girls in china factories who incessantly hurl themselves downstairs with mountains of crockery give me a headache.'

So wrote Franz Kafka in a letter to a friend, when he was working as a clerk for an insurance company. But the same could be said by any barrister who spends his life churning out pleadings on behalf of accident-prone plaintiffs.

Is this the reason for a barrister's procrastination — that his brain is benumbed by drudgery, or the futile wrestling with hopelessly muddled cases? It might, of course, be laziness; or it might be springtime in Lincoln's Inn. Outside his window, the sun lights up the daffodils, tulips and smooth lawns, giving promise of a glorious summer to come.

All of this passes a barrister by unless he has eyes to see. Will the call of spring become so imperious that he flings down his pen with a cry of 'Bother!' and 'O blow!', like the Mole in *The Wind in the Willows*, and dashes out into the golden morning? Can Romance, like a sunbeam, steal across his window-sill? Possibly; a flower already blossoms there. Only a small one, but it is his own.

Procrastination

Portia

There was once a time when A Woman's Place was in the Home. Much determination and many sacrifices were needed before women could take up professional careers. In 1908 it seemed unthinkable that they could ever make their way into the legal profession, at least in the view of F E Smith. He was discussing in the House of Commons the question of Barmaids, rather than maidens at the Bar:

> *FE*: I could give the committee case after case in which respectable women are earning their livings in public-houses for whom no other method of employment could be suggested, and who are supporting relatives. The philanthropists have never suggested any other employment for these women.
>
> *Dr Rutherford* (a Labour MP): Admit them to the legal profession. (Labour cheers)
>
> *FE*: I do not regard the remark of the hon. member as a serious or worthy interruption. (Opposition cheers)

Women have certainly made a serious and worthy entry into the legal profession now. Since judges in the Court of Appeal are by statute 'Lords Justices', the first woman member of that court is entitled 'My Lady Lord Justice Butler-Sloss', an inelegance she does not deserve. Sooner or later there will be a 'Mistress of the Rolls', if that is the appropriate form of words.

Meanwhile, lady barristers stand in the front line of legal warfare, dealing as imperturbably as their male colleagues with the most appalling and intricate cases.

> 'In civilised society', wrote Sir Walter Scott, 'law is the chimney through which all that smoke discharges itself that used to circulate through the whole house, and put everyone's eyes out — no wonder therefore, that the vent itself should sometimes get a little sooty.'

None of the smut rubs off onto Portia. She is too nice a girl.

Portia

The Signing

Signing the will! It has been the centre of many dramas. Charles Mathews QC once cross-examined someone who claimed to have seen the old lady sign it.

Q: Did the defendant put the pen into her hand?
A: Yes.
Q: And assist her while she signed the will?
A: Yes.
Q: How did he assist her?
A: By raising her in the bed and supporting her when he had raised her.
Q: Did he guide her hand?
A: No.
Q: Did he touch her hand at all?
A: I think he did just touch her hand.
Q: When he did touch her hand, WAS SHE DEAD?

The witness fell to the ground in a faint.

A different testator was several kinds of hero. First, a boxing blue. Then he lost his toes on Shackleton's Arctic expedition. He commanded the Life Guards in the First World War, and the Arab Legion in the Second. In later years he lived a little nearer to the world of P G Wodehouse. As Lord Denning said in his judgment:

'Here he was at 85 with only a year or so to go. Alone as he was, he became very eccentric. Take some instances. On one occasion he had all the files about the farms brought up from the tenants' hall and burnt. He said they were rubbish. They included the tenancy agreements. On another occasion he discharged all the employees on the estate. He said they were not earning their keep. But he changed his mind and kept them. His attitude to insurance was unusual, to say the least. He took the line that the insurance company never paid *him* anything, so why should he go on paying *them*.'

He made a new will every four months. Finally, he left his valuable shooting rights to a working man whom he liked and respected. It was claimed that he did not know what he was doing; the claim, happily, failed.

The Signing

The Final Speech

In one of his short stories, Anton Chekhov described the tactics of a defence lawyer.

'He was obviously trying to make it look as if the laundresses had robbed their own laundry. He delivered his speech coolly, angrily eyeing the jury.

He explained burglary and petty larceny. He spoke in great detail and with long conviction, displaying an outstanding talent for expatiating long and solemnly about what was common knowledge. And it was difficult to make out what precisely he *was* getting at. The jurors were able to draw only the following conclusion from his lengthy speech: either there had been a burglary, but no petty larceny, since the money from the sale of the linen was spent by the laundresses on drink; or that there had been larceny, but no burglary.'

This, of course, was fiction. But it was of a real murder trial that Lord Ackner said 'The facts, which I shall shortly recite, disclose a case which even the most charitably minded would be obliged to describe as totally without merit... A surprising variety of possibilities were suggested for the jury's consideration, such as —'. He listed them.

1. That the dead woman had somehow killed herself.
2. That she had been murdered by a stranger.
3. That the defendant had killed her accidentally.
4. That he had killed her in self-defence.
5. That he had killed her under provocation by her.
6. That he had killed her when too drunk to know what he was doing.
7. That he had killed her without intending to do her any serious injury.

The jury acquitted the defendant of murder, and convicted him of manslaughter.

No matter how impassioned the final speech may be, the judge's mind may be elsewhere, for he has heard it all before. This was Mark Twain's verdict on a like situation:

'Of course he oughtn't to go to sleep, because it's shabby; but the finer a person talks the certainer it is to make you sleep, and so when you come to look at it it ain't nobody's fault in particular; both of them's to blame.'

The Final Speech

The Verdict

'I cannot learn that my book hath produced one single effect according to my intentions: judges learned and upright; pleaders honest and modest, with some tincture of common sense; and Smithfield blazing with pyramids of law books.'[1]

Jonathan Swift, *A Letter from Captain Gulliver*

1 Except those published by Butterworths. (Publishers' note)

Acknowledgements and Notes

All the pictures in this book are drawn from imagination, and bear no intended resemblance to any factual legal proceedings, past or present. The same applies to the texts, save for specific references to judges and their judgments.

The extracts from the publications referred to throughout this book are reproduced by kind permission of Penguin Books Ltd, John Calder (Publishers) Ltd, Aitken & Stone Ltd and The Bodley Head.

Point of Departure
Lord Mackay of Clashfern: *R v Sharp (Colin)* [1988] 1 Weekly Law Reports 7, 9.

Femme Fatale
Galdos: 'Episodios Nacionales' I, 224.
Lady Sackville: 'Pepita' by Vita Sackville-West.

Life's Theatre
Lord Justice Woolf: *Burton v Secretary of State for Transport* (1988) Times, 12 February.
Karen Blixen: 'Out of Africa' 1986 Penguin p97.

Time is Money
Charles Dickens: 'The Chimes' (Christmas Books).

Prosecuting Counsel
Cicero: 'On Duties' in 'On the Good Life' translated by M. Grant (1971) Penguin Classics pp146-7.
Anthony Trollope: Mr Chaffenbrass in 'The Three Clerks' said to be modelled on Edwin James QC.

Enter the Clerk
Henry Hawkins: 'A Barrister's Life' in 'Reminiscences' II (1904).

The Young Demosthenes
Seneca: 'Letters from a Stoic' No. 48 translated by R. Campbell (1969) Penguin Classics.

The Conference
Sir Walter Scott: 'Redgauntlet'.

Presenting a Bold Front
George Orwell: 'Collected Essays' Volume 2 Penguin p183.
Baroness Wootton of Abinger: Quoted in the 'Law Guardian',
October 1968.

The Fox
The Spanish Novel: F. de Quevedo 'The Swindler' in 'Two Spanish
Picaresque Novels' translated by R. Wilks (1972) Penguin Classics.
The American Film: Billy Wilder's 'The Fortune Cookie'.
Lord Justice Croom-Johnson: *R v Southwark Coroner ex parte Hicks*
[1987] 1 Weekly Law Reports 1624, 1630, 1635.

A Good Result
J. Arbuthnot: 'Law is a Bottomless Pit' — This is the work in which
John Bull first appeared.
Sir Walter Scott: 'Guy Mannering', and in his 'Journal' 12
December, 1825.
Lord Simon of Glaisdale: *Central Asbestos Co Ltd v Dodd* [1972] 3
Weekly Law Reports 333, 353.
Franz Kafka: 'Letters to Friends Family and Editors' translated by
Richard and Clara Winston (1978) John Calder.

Portia
Sir Walter Scott: 'Guy Mannering'.

The Signing
Charles Matthews QC: In Henry Hawkin's 'Reminiscences' II (1904).
Lord Denning: *Re Brocklehurst's Estate* [1977] 3 Weekly Law
Reports 696.

The Final Speech
Anton Chekhov: 'Three Years' in 'The Fiancée and Other Stories'
translated by R. Wilks (1986) Penguin Classics p137.
Lord Ackner: *R v Saunders* [1987] 3 Weekly Law Reports 355, 358.
Mark Twain: 'Tom Sawyer Abroad'.